For Joseph and Gabriel
who were tiny and grew big—N. D.

WRITTEN BY NICOLA DAVIES

For Lex and Kit —E. S.

TINY CREATURES

The World of Microbes

ILLUSTRATED BY EMILY SUTTON

CANDLEWICK PRESS

You know about big animals,

and you know about small animals . . .

but do you know that there are creatures so tiny
that millions could fit on this ant's antenna?

So tiny that we'd have to make the ant's antenna
as big as a whale to show them to you?

ANTENNA

They don't have eyes,
heads, or legs,
branches, roots, or
leaves because they
aren't animals or plants.
But they are alive.

They are called
microbes,
and there are lots of them.

A single drop of
seawater can hold
twenty million microbes.
That's about the same
as the number of people
in New York State.

And a teaspoon of soil can have
as many as a **billion** microbes.
That's about the same as the number
of people in the whole of India.

Microbes live everywhere—in the sea, on land, in the soil, and in the air. They live in places where nothing else does, like in volcanoes, or inside rocks, or at the back of your fridge.

They also live on the outside and inside of plants and animals.

Right now there are more microbes living on your skin than there are people on Earth, and there are ten or even a hundred times as many as that in your stomach.

(Don't worry! Although some microbes make you sick, the ones that live in you and on you all the time help keep you well.)

But even though they are too small to see, they are not all the same. There are lots of different kinds, more than there are different kinds of animals and plants. Some are tinier than others, as different in size as ants and whales.

● ←—— POLIO VIRUS
One of the smallest microbes

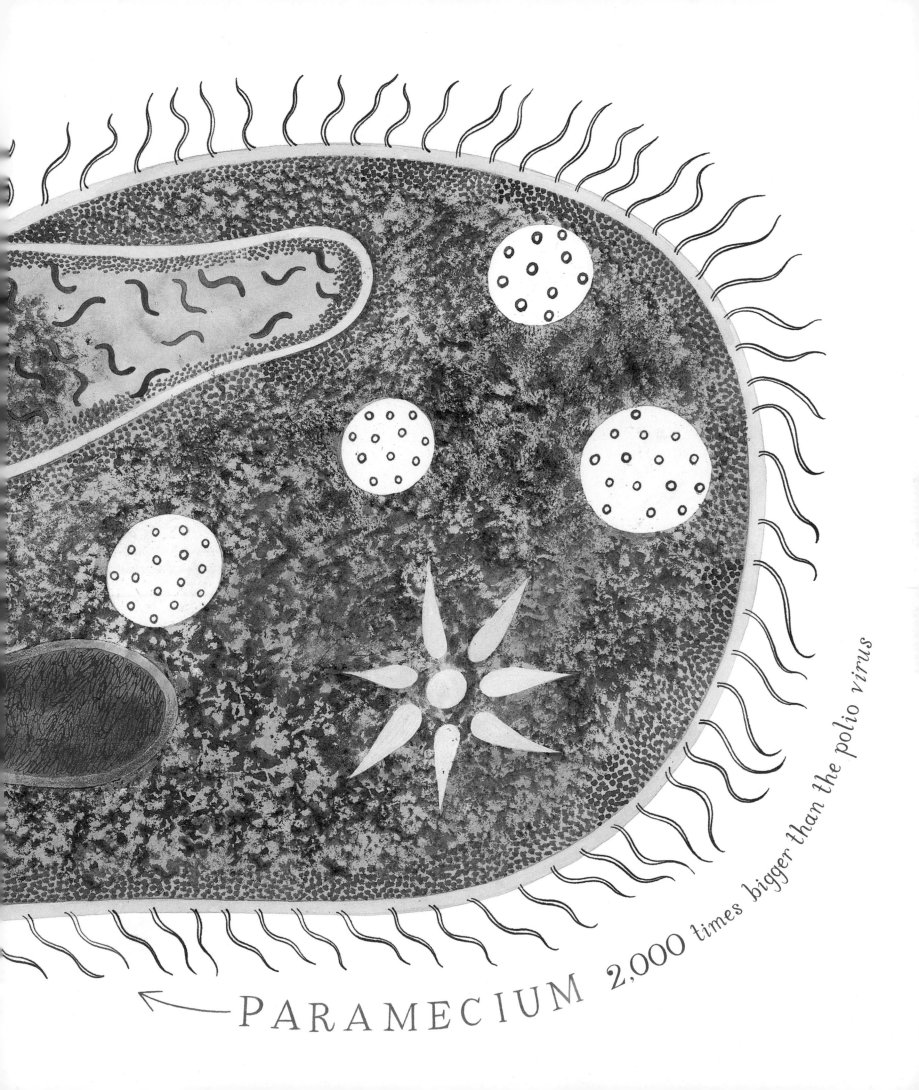

← PARAMECIUM 2,000 *times bigger than the polio virus*

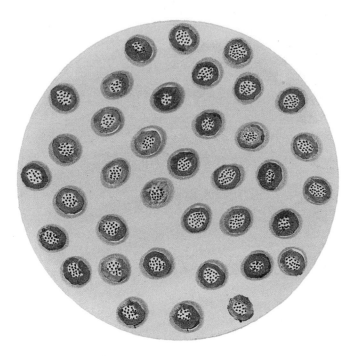

Some microbes are round.

Some are skinny.

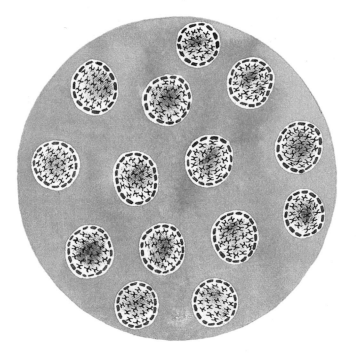

Some look like shells.

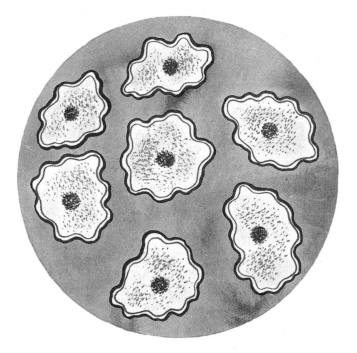

Some are squishy.

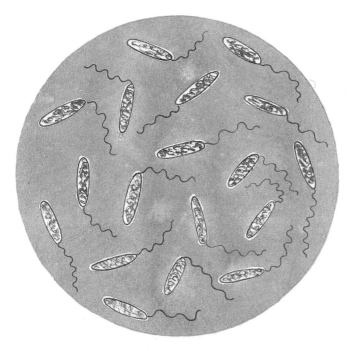

Some have wiggling tails.

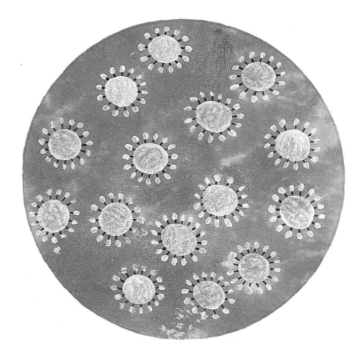

Some look like daisies.

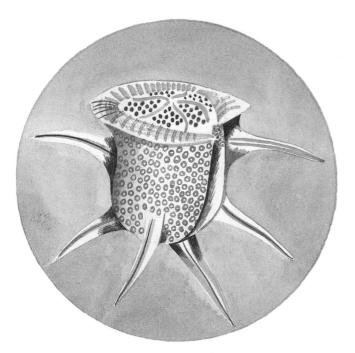

Some look like spaceships.

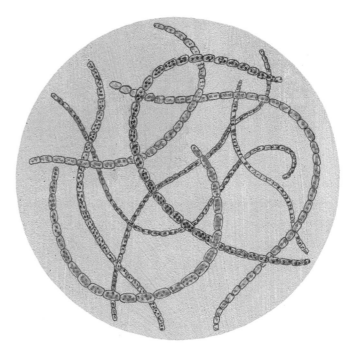

Some look like necklaces.

Microbes can eat anything: plants, animals (alive or dead), even oil and rocks. They're too small to have mouths, so they just soak up what they need through their skin.

MENU
PLANTS
—
ANIMALS
—
ROCKS
—
OIL

That's why the things microbes eat
don't disappear in bites. They change,
slowly, into something else. . . .

FOOD *INTO* COMPOST

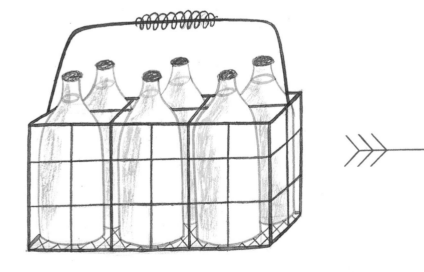 

MILK *INTO* YOGURT

ROCKS *INTO*
SOIL

And when microbes are well fed, they are really,
really good at making more microbes.
They simply split, so that where there was one,

twenty minutes later, there are two . . .

and then four,

and then eight,

and then sixteen.

Starting with just one microbe of a type
called E. coli, which of course would be far
too small for you to see, it would take eleven
and a half hours for there to be enough E. coli

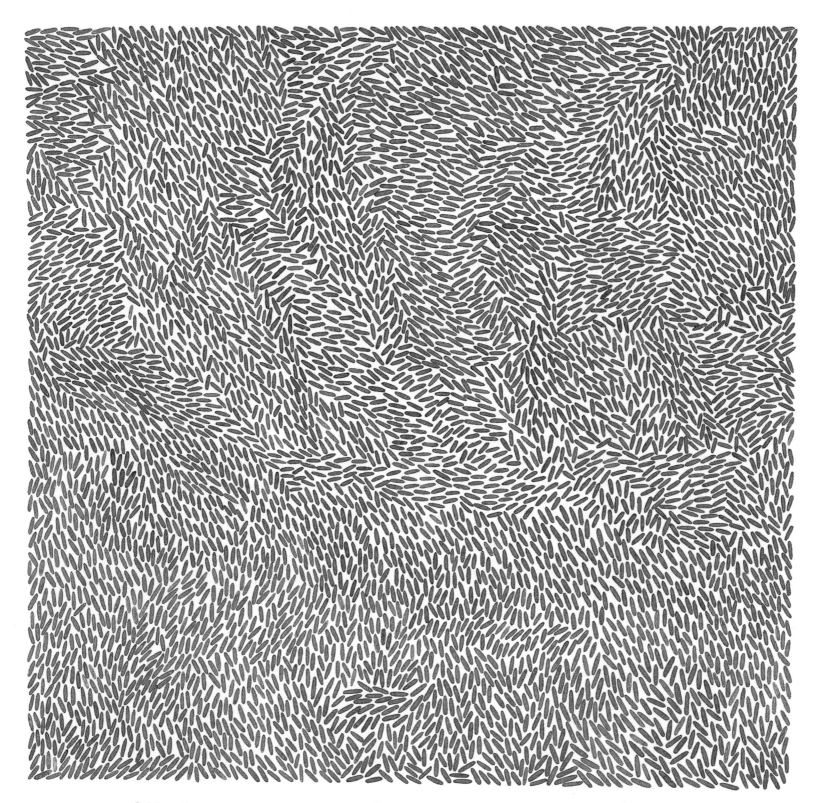

to fill this space, and twenty minutes later . . .

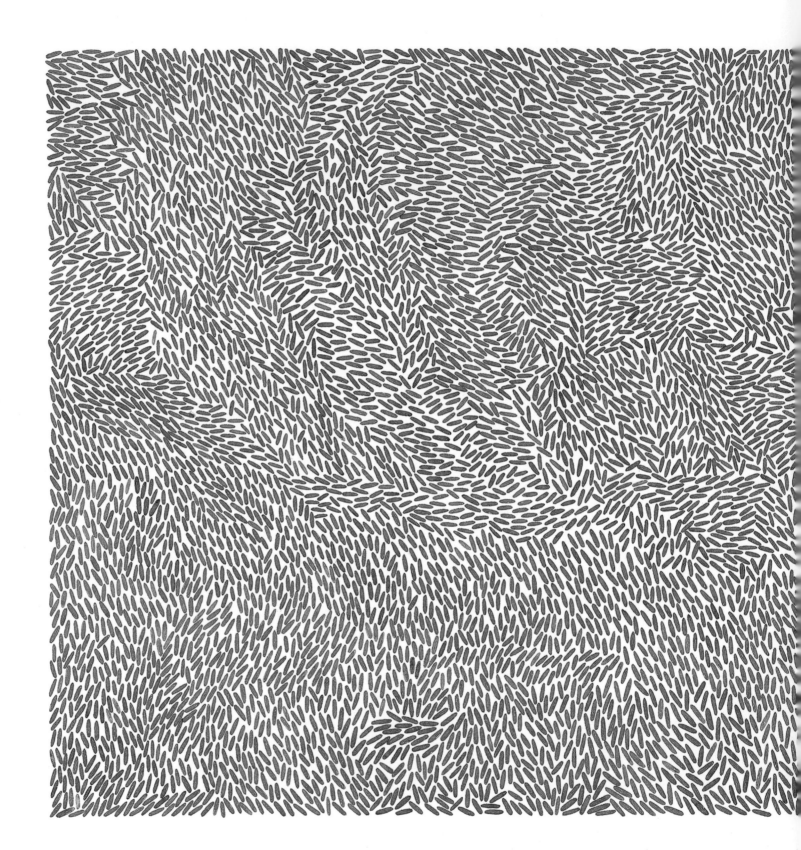

they would all split and

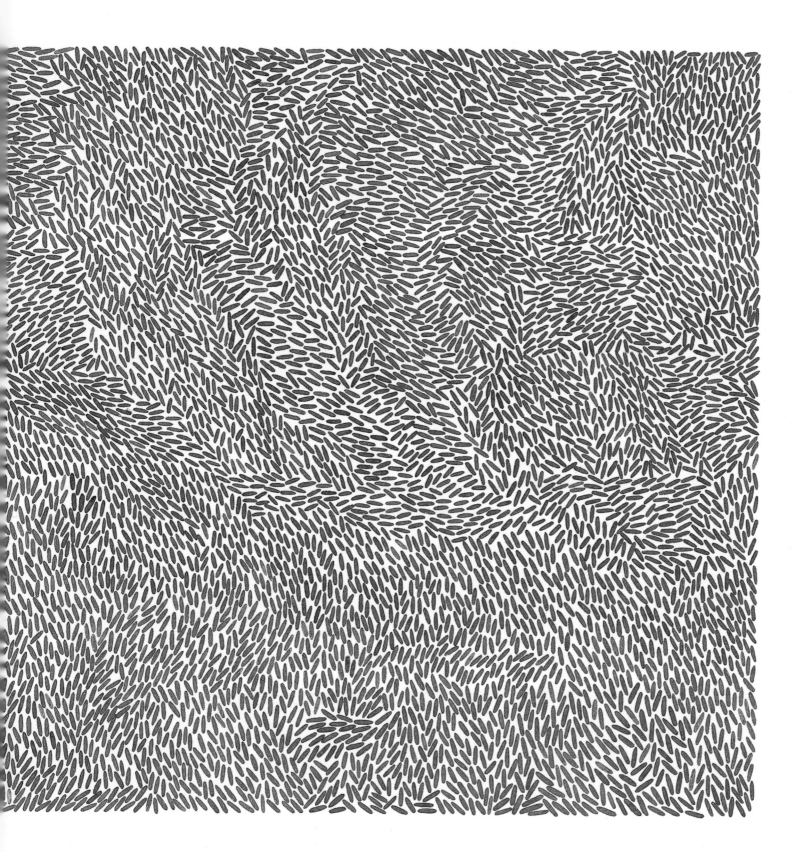

double, to fill this space.

That's why it takes only a few
of the wrong kind of microbes—
the kind we call germs—
to get into your body to make you sick.

←MOSQUITO

They get in through
your mouth or through a cut
or sometimes through an insect's bite.
Then, inside you, where they are warm and well fed,
they split and split and split until just a few germs
have turned into thousands, then millions.
They're still tiny, but there are enough
of them to make you sick.

So it's best to stop them from getting in.

Luckily, only a few kinds of microbes can make humans sick.
Most microbes are busy doing other things.

And because microbes are so
good at making more microbes,
some of the things they do
are very, very big.

They can wear down mountains
and build up cliffs.
They can stain the sea red,
turn the sky cloudy,
and make snowflakes grow.

They recycle everything that dies to make soil so that new life can sprout, and they help to make our air good to breathe.

All over the earth,
all the time, tiny microbes
are eating and eating,
and splitting and splitting,
changing one thing into another.
They are the invisible
transformers of our world—

the tiniest lives doing some
of the biggest jobs.